Nov 2016

D1221169

Kansas City, MO Public Lib

00001833893197

THE ABRIDGED HISTORY
OF RAINFALL

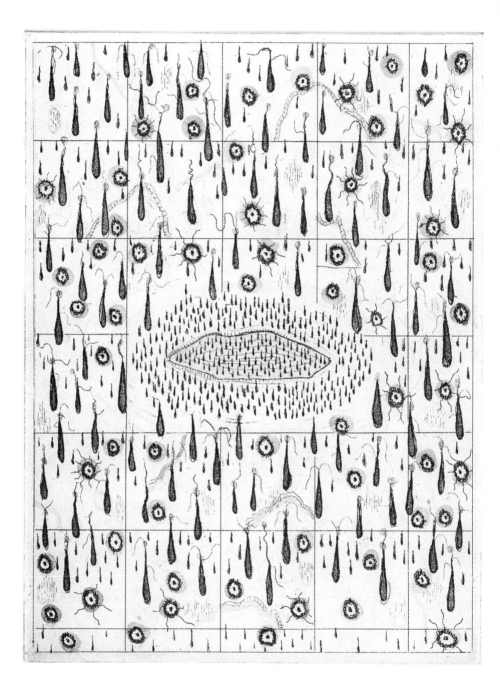

THE
ABRIDGED
HISTORY OF
RAINFALL

JAY HOPLER

McSWEENEY'S
POETRY SERIES

McSWEENEY'S

SAN FRANCISCO

Copyright © 2016 Jay Hopler

Cover design and illustration by Sunra Thompson.

Frontispiece: "Rain Table" by Tony Fitzpatrick.

All rights reserved, including right of reproduction in whole or part, in any form.

The McSweeney's Poetry Series is edited by Dominic Luxford and Jesse Nathan.

The editors wish to thank assistant editor Rachel Z. Arndt,
editorial interns Waylon Elder, Megan Freshley, Tikva Hecht,
and Linnea Ogden, and copyeditor Britta Ameel.

Special thanks to Jeremy Rishel. The publication of this book
would not have been possible without his support.

McSweeney's and colophon are registered trademarks of McSweeney's,
a privately held company with wildly fluctuating resources.

Printed in the United States.

ISBN 978-1-944211-26-4

2   4   6   8   10   9   7   5   3   1

www.mcsweeneys.net

for my father,
Robert Sherwood Hopler
1927–2009

CONTENTS

I.

II.

III.

once more a world of lamentation in which
all things that were, were once more near: forest and gorge
and path and village, field and brook and beast;
and that around this weeping world,
as around the other earth, a sun
turned and a silent, starry heaven,
a heaven of lamentation filled with disfigured stars—:
                                                    —Rainer Maria Rilke

I.

WINTER NIGHT FULL OF STARS

I am a winter night full of stars. I am that star, the one you
  thought was a plane.
I am the shadow of that plane casting its blackness over the
  lake house like a
Shroud. And I am that shroud, black, embroidered
With stars, under which you grew cold that January
Night, laid out upon your catafalque
Of down.

                                    And those feathers
Were as snow in that mortuary air—, floated like snowflakes
  in that mortuary air
When the wind came up. And when the wind died down,
They were as snow upon
The ground.

Am I the smoke drifting through the bare branches
Of a Japanese maple—, or am I the Japanese maple, smoke
  drifting through its bare branches?
It is not smoke, but light burning
To a fine ash. And in that darkness, may you, like those dark
  blooms, shine. Come, O—
Let us to dust
Together.

WHERE IS ALL THIS WATER COMING FROM?

Another dull, unrainy day.
Not warm. Not cool. A little wind, then none.
My mother turns a light on
    And sits down on the sofa with a book.
        A blue jay lights for an instant
            On the back fence. Some clouds wisp by.
            Or is that smoke? Some smoke wisps by.
        Bright, though distant,
                The sound of gunfire. Or a car backfiring.
                On the air, the smell of wet wood burning.
But that can't be——. All day
The clouds have rolled their grim lead
            Westward and left us…nothing.
            I wonder what she's reading.
            The Unabridged History
        Of Rainfall. No, it's Günter Eich,
   Botschaften des Regens. That book, when read
By a widow, in her marriage house, aloud, and in the German,
        Makes a man want
            To turn his eyes sky-
        Ward and confide
            His despair to the migrating
            Birds. If only there were migrating
                Birds.

SELF-PITY IS BETTER THAN
NO PITY AT ALL

When the moon's white push unplumbs the sunflower,
The yellow mums behind my father's house disappear
In a combustion of butterflies. Too bad
I am not a lover of butterflies.

                                    Such a rowdy hallelujah
Is wasted on me. Even so—, I don't think it would be
Such a bad thing, disappearing

                        In a combustion of butterflies.
It would be better than staying in this ghostly house
With nothing to keep me company but these yellow
Mums and butterflies.

                              That crooked sunflower.
And that moon. That pushy, pushy
Moon.

IT WAS NOT OF THE MOON
WE DREAMT

But of the moon's reflection
In the riggings of the fishing smacks

And of the moon's reflection
In the tin roofs of the fishing shacks

And of the moon's reflection
In the black eyes of the island cats

That sat beside the fishermen
And watched them bait their grapples.

—————

We never dreamt the moon
A map of earthly absences,

Those fish-foul towns
By tides destroyed, those slips where

Once this fishing fleet rode
Berth. And yet…,

—————

Just so: a map: that chanticleer of chandeliers, the
    moon, strutting for his henny harem of houselights
And lighthouses.

UMBRIAN ANECDOTES

Every evening, at sunset, a company of green parakeets leaves the
    fig trees in the garden
And flies east, over Assisi,
Or flies west—over Assisi.

When they fly east, they fly chattering, pieces of ripe fig falling
    from their orange beaks.
When they fly west, they fly chattering, pieces of ripe fig falling
    from their orange beaks.

Every evening, at sunset, these parakeets fly, pieces of ripe fig
    falling in the garden,
Or in the streets of Assisi,
To the west or to the east.

Later, the fig trees empty of parakeets, the moon come full and low,
The garden stretches itself in every direction—. Towards Assisi.

A church bells the birds

Over the roofs of Perugia and a blue haze in a gauze-fall sprawls
    along the walls; the sun

'S light hits not hard the hills, but holds
Them. Still—.

                And stills their green velocity.

O, THE SADNESS IMMACULATE

The women in Rome are so beautiful
It's like being beaten to death in slow motion
Looking at them—; it's like bleeding.

So I don't look at them.

I look at the parakeets nesting in the blood
Orange trees, the moon rising behind some ancient
    something-or-other, the first few stars.

From my window, I can see the house
Where Galileo invented the telescope.

I wonder what he was thinking
That night, that night he first searched
Heaven. I wonder what it was

He was trying not to see.

NOT ALL SKELETONS ARE
MUSEUM QUALITY

Under a sky as hazy-blue-polluted
As the late-August air in Rome, the clouds with the frayed hems

Of their white skirts dipped in smoke,
The birds with their dingy wingspans;

From an oak tree, its trunk warped
By a hundred years and more of wars

And storms, its lowest, thickest limbs stripped bare so as to give the
    executioner more room to
String the ropes—; in a death-burlesque

Of marionettes, their hands tied fast before them,
The frayed hems of their white shirts enthreaded
On the wind,

Twenty-one men are hanging.

———————

CRUSHED BY THE SKY!

That would be the headline—; and every olive tree in this garden
Would weep its leaves, its silver-green-gray leaves, like a widow weeps

Its glass when a rock sails through
It. I mean a *window*.

Shatter—, *shatter*—, say the bells
Of Santa Maria in Trastevere. *When you're lost, you're gone forever,*

Say the birds. *Dreadful sorry,*
Say the clementines—

———

A perfect Wedgwood Jasper sky, a few high clouds in white relief—.
The *giardinieri* are cutting down one of the park's older oaks.

Axe-thwack and chainsaw-
Rev. The thunk and crack

Of branches hitting brick and splitting. Crows shower out from the
        oak's listing crown
And black the sky

A moment before vanishing.

———

The sun so high and full over the garden.
And so bright.

A MORAL VICTORY IS
STILL A DEFEAT

It was the twenty-first of January,
And in Sant'Agnese in Agone
The light was not quite right.
    So late in January,

It should have been a watery amber
Dripping through those high dome
Windows. Instead, it was a smoldered orange,
    Almost embered,

And it rose from the floor
In front of the altar, a kind of shimmer
That made of Guidi's *Holy Family* an inferior mirage.
    That rose someone left on the floor

In front of the altar,
Was that where the light was coming from?
Was it coming from those candles burning
    On the altar?

No. It was from the shrine that light
Came shining, from the skull of the saint herself!
How dismal the winter that year,
    Rome steeped in a weak-tea light.

As though the world
Were trapped in amber. O, Agnes, it was—
It was trapped in amber.
    The sorry world.

POEM WRITTEN ON THE FIRST ANNIVERSARY OF MY FATHER'S DEATH

Curled on sacks of cypress mulch, their bodies slack
    with sleep, two cats:
One black, one a dirty gray,
Both scrawny and flea-foul.

    When a boy
Rides by on his pawn-shop
Bike, yelling and knocking over garbage cans,

They do not lift their heads.
They do not lift their heads
When the thunder drops its load of stones into the
    rain barrel. Not even the wind,

Honed on the hinges
Of foreclosure signs, has edge enough
To cut them from such sleep

As they have found; not even the rain
When it comes—if it comes—
Will trouble them.

AFTER THE OBSEQUIES, ETC.

On the pond beyond the north lawn,
    Swans in honking congress congregate.
The gates of the estate are chained, the manor's curtains drawn.
On the pond beyond the north lawn,
The breeze has thrown a sheet of leaves and then withdrawn
    To tend the family cemetery. Who leaves graves in such a state?
On the pond beyond the north lawn,
    Swans in honking congress congregate,
        Echoes of all that here was elegant
            And fine. Elegant? Try: obnoxious. Forget *lamentations,*
        Flocks of swans are *dins*! If only noise could slow the sun's descent!
        Echoes of all that here was elegant
        Die across the darkling firmament.
            A breeze sweeps leaves from a grave's chipped face. On that
                stone, an epitaph: *Forget your lamentations!*
            An echo of all that here was elegant
                And fine? Try: obnoxious. Try: impossible.

EULOGY (CURRENTLY IN REVISION)

To jump in the hole. To sleep like gold.
To kiss the fishnets and the crabpots and the quay.
To prick the cricket, to prick the cricket.
No. To pry open its one good eye.

To have one good eye, how lucky!
To fold the clothes. To fold the clothes.
To fill the codpiece with buckshot
And drop it.

      To ride bareback on the white rabbit.
Father, O!—, to ride bareback!

To unmonkey the huzzah and sizzle
Like the inkpot firebomb. No,
Like the gunpowder wingspan.
To sizzle.

MEDITATION ON A POEM
CURRENTLY IN REVISION

Gone the cherubim and the cherry bomb—the porch-lit
    orchid and the orchard of porcelain.
Gone the wind-flogged tapestries, the ashen baptistery with
    its fiery doors ajar.

Gone the Key cock with its coral-orange comb!
Gone the grande dame with her corset of bone—

————

No longer stalks the farmhand his boss's star-lit field.
No longer sleeps the foxhound by the river.

              And all the bells cry, *No longer! No longer!*
Until there are no longer any bells and all

That under Heaven is
Falls quiet.

————

          Fire! Fire!
That pot of ink in the original still sizzles—
That inkpot firebomb!

————

No horse-drawn coffin, no coffee plantation, no Roman
    bone church,
No fleas in amber, no decommissioned reliquary.

No rogue Ferris wheel
Shrieking down streets

                  Warm with corpses.

SONNET ON CONSEQUENCE

O, those smells!
The throbbing, wet, and fleshy smells; the thin, brittle-limber

Smells; the smells that rose like smoke, edgy and tendrilled,
From behind the high hedgerows! I tried so hard to believe

Those smells were indispensable, an understanding of their
 intricacies
Necessary not only for a more intelligent and sophisticated

Appreciation of the natural world, but also for a more agile,
More passionate reckoning of our relationship to the world

In general, to its gifts and limitations—.

————

Unfortunately,

I couldn't make myself believe those smells were anything
More than pleasant addenda to an early evening's walk—

Bloom-woozy and full of swoon, maybe…but necessary?
No, not necessary. Not for understanding this world, anyway.

————

And what other world is there?

MAY 25

Behind the banyan trees, the mansions. Behind the mansions,
     the lagoon—.
In the lagoon, a mooring of sailboats.

Wind in the rigging.
Hull-slap and groan.

                              Where is everybody?

The sound of people playing in their pools—well…, there
Isn't any; the streets

Are empty—, the moon, like a moon
Jelly, beating its slow float in the not-

Quite-dark. In the gardens of the Moorings Country Club,
The lights have come on, rice paper lanterns

Printed with cherry blossoms. O—this un-
Starred sky. And the smell of the star

Jasmine, the fleshy, resplendent scent
Of the gardenia. Is this where I say, *I*

Miss you? Where I say, *Father, isn't there anything*
In this evening's long cortege of bloom as beautiful

                              As it used to be?

Like the sound of an empty ship drifting
Through fog—like a sweet-despicable

Imitation of mourning—a piteousness of doves
Is cooing in the banyan trees.

II.

EXCERPTS FROM THE UNABRIDGED HISTORY OF RAINFALL

In dark rain and sharp rain.
In this rain-sharpened dark.
In this dark sharpened by the sound of rain falling on the
    roof of the hospital.
In blessèd rain.
In godless rain.
In rain that lays its gray weight on the grass.
In rain that passes through the branches of the aspen and the
    mountain ash
And of this drip-lit river
Makes a testament
To Heaven's
Lack of light.

———

Your doctor with his every room a shadeless chandelierium,
    what is this dark but light unlamped
To him?

———

In the photograph, my father is running down Miami Beach,
    his feet kicking up fans of sand between the splayed legs
    of lithe, smiling University of Miami cheer-
Leaders. The year is 1947; God has, once again,
Cast Satan from His Heaven and it is safe to turn one's face
    unto the sun. The palm fronds by sea breezes

Bent are black against the thunder–
Headed sky. The hull of every sailboat is white.
At the edge of the beach, an empty bench, birds—

———————

After the German (I)

From the hedgerow

The call of the plover, as plaintive
As it is strong. You think of Saint Jerome:
There is in this one voice such an intense loneliness,
Only a downpour

Could answer it.

———————

Forget about your bones,
This wet gets in the *soul*,

The *spirit*, whatever you
Want to call it, that pilot

Light we're all so proud
Of, and makes you wish

Its sad dim flame would
Just hiss out—the water-

Logged fronds of the tin
Palms dripping, the gate

Swinging, sodden, on its
Hinge.

—————

After the German (II)

Nothing will there be but rain—,
No roof and no dam will protect me from it—,
On the paths will be trampled
Spring's green to muck.

—————

The gray sky collapsing like a lung—

—————

                    The thunder down its heavy leather
Lays and from the ruined garden by the lake a hazy
        murmuration lifts into the rain-lit
Air, blurs into the mists that swirl there,

Then settles in thin wing-swept breaths
Back

Into the maidenhair.

———————

After the German (III)

In the hospital, the suffering howl.
The night's bluish plumage buzzes.
The rain, glittering, thunders down
Upon the roofs.

———————

The streetlights have come on.
Soon, it will be dark

Enough to see them.

———————

Today it rained so hard, Father.
You could hear it, life's shortness

Of breath.

BIRDS ARE HOW THE EARTH
MAKES SENSE OF HEAVEN

A flock of songbirds, icterine, eyes black as overcast
Angels' has overwhelmed

                                        The orange tree
That grows so near the house its branch tips tap the
        tempered glass
Of the kitchen's picture window. Were it possible

To overlook such a raucous congregation, to look past
        that mass of bodies heliotic, sung-and-burned,
The sky thickening into storm might intend toward the
        magnitudes of the apparent, the apparent

Magnitude of a star like Wormwood
Or the sun; or, it might not. It might

                                        Present, instead,
A leaden version of the ethereal, an elemental Heaven,
        grave-dark and clumsy
Under its own gray

Weight.

                        ———

                        But—, there's no getting past those things.
Even if one were deaf and colorblind, eyes like theirs...
        not even Ramiel

Had eyes like theirs and he was
The Thunder of God. If only it were possible

To see this world

As those creatures see it! Might not the rain, then, for all
    down-fallen things a formless
Sort of sympathy elicit? Might

Not this kitchen's window be an illustration called

            An Oriel of Aureoles / An Aureole of Orioles

Its glass a flash so bright, so yellow…, like the birds
    themselves had been the stain,
The oxide in the pot metal?

               ———

                         It might and it might
Be——. Still, black as are those eyes, a landscape à la Bosch
    (say: *Christ*
In Limbo) seems more likely, a scene ripped,
Mean and screaming,

          From Bruegel's *The Triumph*

Of Death.

ELEGY FOR THE LIVING

It's not that today was beautiful; it's that today was too beautiful.
It was a day so beautiful, it made you afraid God would notice it

And, having noticed it, would notice you, living in it, would see
You sitting there, lounging on your back deck, sipping whiskey,

Unslapped and happy (at last!) in your boredom and anonymity,
And remember that He hates you, that, of all His creations, you

Are the least impressive, the least likeable, the one on whom all
Grace is wasted and the one from whom His kindness should be kept.

                                                      That's why,
When a flock of yellow songbirds takes up choir in the branches

Of the orange tree, you throw stones at them, curse them into the air,
Into someone else's sphere—

    Your songs upon the neighbors
    God's attention call;
    Let God regret the neighbors
    For a while!

THE GROVE

Like unborn suns in bunches hung from branches bent by
    years spent holding up such pulp-plump fruit,
Gorgeous and corpulent, their green rinds tight
And shining, sheened with rain, the season's first blood
Oranges are on the trees.

How beautiful they would look against a blue
Sky! How weary they look against this black
One—.

To be born tired and to live tired and to die tired.
To die of tiredness. Not as hard to imagine as it used to be.
    Was ever there a sky this low?
No, and still there's not.
It's just a flock of black-

Birds shrouding out above the trees. The moon
Is up there…somewhere.
And the stars.

THE RANGES OF BIRDS

A simple spiritless *per-wee* or *chu-wee*.

A staccato *tuk-a-tuk* or *kut-a-kut*; also a single *kewk*.

A piercing *wheep!* or *kleep!*; a loud *pic, pic, pic*.

    A low nasal *wurk*; also *check, check, check*.

    A hoarse *kar-wit, kar-wit*. When flushed, a cackle.

A cackling *kor-ee-ee-a, kor-ee-ee-a*.

An emphatic sneezy bark, *kee-yow!*, *wow!*, or *waow!*

An asthmatic squeal, *keeer-r-r* (slurring downward).

    A slightly phoebelike *p-p-pit-zee* or *pit-a-zee*.

    A croaking *cr-r-ruck* or *prruk*; a metallic *tok*.

A harsh *tseeeer*; a whistled *whooee*.

A musical *teew*; also a rattle and a whistle, *ticky-tick-tew*.

A throaty, rasping *za-za-za*; also *kay-weck, kay-weck*.

    A nasal *wide-a-wake* or *wacky-wack*.

    A loud whistled *wheeep!* Also a rolling *prrrrreet!*

BEAUTY IS A REAL THING, I'VE SEEN IT

If only those parakeets would settle
A little nearer to where I'm sitting, instead of at the tops of far-off
    trees, this morning
Would be so much more remarkable.
One could watch the blackbirds, I suppose, peck their ways like
    Oxford dons across
The flagstone paths and lawns, or the swallows, or the sparrows,
Or the crows. But those birds are so plain—, so…painfully
    available.
No, only those parakeets will do and they will not do
What I want them to. In this, they are like everything else in the
    world.
Every beautiful thing.

WHAT THIS POEM MEANS

This poem means it thunders too much—, nothing coming of it.

This poem means it is the End of Days, Sunshine—. We're all
    going to snuff it in the dark and when we do, the angels will,
    like murderbirds, descend on us from Heaven, our prayers still
    caught in their teeth.

This poem means whether you are loved or left, whether you
    love or leave, the only things that change are the names of
    your creditors.

This poem means the bells of the ruined church on the corner
    are chiming the Cambridge Quarters a little too slowly and a
    little too late.

This poem means there are no pear trees in the monastery's
    anatomically correct apple orchard.

This poem means I'm so miserable my stars shine on Jesus!

This poem means I burn like an exaggerated candle.

This poem means the wind whops the shutters shut, the
    parakeets keening in the blood orange trees.

ALARUMS. FLOURISHES. EXEUNT.

A dog doth to itself give yelpèd bliss, but you and I are not such
    things as bliss, self-yelped, doth well suffice
These days. You know I'd suffer for you, if I could.
Is that a radio playing? If only you could get out of bed, sit by
    the window—. If only you could hear it.

                           Hear it?

Our song is changing its bird bones.

————

What yelpèd bliss a dog doth give itself! If only you and I such
    bliss possessed. Wouldn't that suffice?
Someday—, no. Someday isn't coming—. But there is a radio
    playing. If you could just get out of bed, make
It to the window—. If only you could hear it.

                           Hear it:

Our only song has changed its bones.

FROM A WINDOW

I saw the hooded crow lift from the
Back wall and fly south, over the village, toward the river.

I saw, her apron sacked with apples,
The caretaker's daughter come slowly in from the orchard.

I saw the thunderheads bloom in an
Otherwise clear sky and drift, low. And darken the garden.

———————

Clouds of flies in the Roman pines are by the breeze and a
    mistling rain
Unshaped, reshaped, unshaped
Again, while the autumn sky like a gray robe lowers and the
    mowers, cold
And tired of being wet, linger just inside the doorway
Of a weather-beaten shed telling jokes in *romanaccio*
And smoking hand-rolled
Cigarettes—

———————

I saw by the back gate the caretaker
Stoop to stroke the stray cat and give to it his dish of food.

I saw one by one the vesper candles
Lit behind the stained-glass windows of the village chapel.

                              I saw the olive trees, their branches
Strung with drips, shudder in a sudden gust and, of the air,

———————

A prism make of drops.

———————

And so it was the autumn light, sawed by drops of water,
Refracted into flights of

Flashes; spectral flames—

ELEGY

From the tall brown grass, a small brown bird appears.
    A woodcock. Or is it a heath hen? It hops
To the middle of the field and stands,
Its tiny eyes shining even in the faint,
Uneven evening light
Of autumn.

GLOSE

Mine is a world foregone though not yet ended,—
An imagined garden grey with sundered boughs
And broken branches, wistful and unmended,
And mist that is more constant than all vows.

—Hart Crane, from "Postscript"

Aside from being likewise father-fraught
And likewise fond of booze and likewise not from Mother in
    any way defended,
And though I have said, as you have said:
Mine is a world foregone though not yet ended,—

And though we those manias, their subsequent depressions, share,
And though it's true that I, like you, am given to a certain
    humid, tropical carouse
And fetishize O Carib Isles lush, and though I, too, live in
An imagined garden grey with sundered boughs

And am haunted by my history, the path
I've through this blooming world cut (such brooders, we! such
    splendid
Sufferers! Two trees we are with crooked trunks
And broken branches, wistful and unmended),

I am nothing like you, Mr. Crane. I will not fail.
I will not fall like garbage from some ship's slick deck, its bow's
Great wake raking mares' manes from the spume
And mist that is more constant than all vows.

THE PALLBEARER

O, wet-black, gleaming sequin
   Factory, a.k.a.: "you starry night,"
   What's with all the strobe-bright
Ornament? This is a coffin

Not some diva's palanquin
   I'm carrying. You get that, right—
O, wet-black, gleaming sequin
   Factory, a.k.a.: "you starry night"?

Can't you be like these banyans?
   Ungrieving, but seemly…, polite.
   It's my father, for the love of Christ!
The new moon is finally risen.

A wet-black, gleaming sequin.

JAZZ FUNERAL

Blame our lack of fatted apples on these lachrymose battledores.
On these flame-retardant peach carts, blame our mania for sleep.

O, fatherless, O sunlit jumper cables! O cancerous chandeliers!
Blame our spermicidal honeymoon on these inebriated bicycles.

On these phosphorescent pestles, blame our addiction to prisms.
On these plum-colored thunderheads, blame our flight from ink.

O cadaverous handstands! O firm, O beachfront cummerbunds!
Blame our sung-burned tongues on these fleet and morbid orgies.

CLOUD CHANTY

The sun is on the muscle and the heat is in the trees.
A fleet of East Indiamen adrift in the doldrums, that's what
The clouds look like. Robot wasps! Look out!

Two helicopters are hovering over the harbor,
That is to say. Their downwash caps the water white.
The sun is on the muscle and the heat is in the trees—

This summer sky's so blue, it almost vibrates.
What's the worst that could happen? We die, that's what!
The clouds look like plow horses. *Look out*

Yonder to the beet fields, Laddie—goes the old
Song, almost a hymn—*the girls are in their dresses white!*
The sun is on the muscle and the heat is in the trees,

So what's with all the shivering? Plague doctors,
Their white beaks scything through the blue air, that's what
The clouds look like. Mechanized lionfish! Look out!

Two prawn trawlers are crawling toward the harbor,
That is to say—, their bow-thrown wakes churned white.
The sun is on the muscle and the heat is in the trees.
The clouds look like ... shrouds? Look out—

III.

EPIGRAPH

Every year at about this time,
I pull the vines from the back
Fence, replace any boards that might
Be split and oil the hinges on

The gate. I cannot tell you
How many years I have done
This.

       Last year when I did this,
My father was alive.

THE ROOSTER KING

Till Armageddon no Shalam, no Shalom,
Then the father hen will call his chickens home.
                                        —Johnny Cash

1.

Another Gorgeous Day in Florida

This afternoon makes me think I will die badly.
One minute, it's cloudy, the next, the sun is so

Bright, it's like having your brains pecked out.
This afternoon makes me think I will die badly.

Oak trees, tea roses, Spanish moss.... A small
Hawk from the dogwood drops its shadow on

The late-June lawn. Blue baskets fat with red
Blooms flank the stone steps to the front porch.

This afternoon makes me think I will die badly.
I want to die badly! Drunk and bloody, crying

For my mother, pleading with God to save me—.
But, this afternoon, I'm happy. Why shouldn't

I be? I'm not some murdered bird, some chicken
Kicked to its pitiful death in a vacant lot. I'm

Not some waste of a perfectly lovely afternoon.
A tea rose, is there anything more excruciating?

This afternoon makes me think I will die badly.
Is it the way the crepe myrtle catches the shadow

Of the hawk in the pink folds of its petal dress?
Is it the way the lawn laps at the front steps, its

Rough mane lashing? A breeze moves through.
Church bells ring the quarter-hour. On the ends

Of thick, green stems, the hips of breeze-blown
Roses float, exhausted, spent as wrecked comets.

This afternoon makes me think I will die badly.
Please, God, let it happen! A palm rat scratches

In the lavender. A wild rooster cocks his throat
And crows.

2.

A Valediction: Forbidding Mourning

      Like a despot resplendent in his dress reds,
His iridescent epaulettes glowing, gloried in the Yborian morning,

A rooster, standing beneath the avocado tree.
How puissant he looks, how regal in the leaf-

Dapple. Not even a kick delivered by some cruel kid could make a
  cock that kingly cower.
He is Fat Sam, Lord of the Gorgeous! He crows the world open.
  That sound, like a screen door being twisted off its hinges—

And the way he stalks that vacant lot,
The sun behind him, rising, his every

Feather flaring like a blood-fingered grease fire, a bottle rocket
Atom bomb—he's Sennacherib come to Babylon! Lightning flying

    From his Assyrian slings—

Cue the bagpipes! Cue the drummers! Let upon the streets be
Flung conniptions of chrysanthemums! Let rose petals be flung

From the rooftops of the burned-out cigar factories, the ruined
  breweries,
The derelict warehouses haunted with cobwebs. Have we not

For this day hard-praying been, our radiance fraying
Even as our voices rose

                    To hit those strident high notes? Is this
Not the key and the ignition, the *Will* and the *Be* and the *Done*?

3.

Note to Self

The evening sky is streaking violet, orange, peach above the hovelled shotgun shacks and abandoned factories.

A cock is crowing.

That sound is nothing like Bishop's "grating of a wet match," nothing like Tate's "dark blue velvet." It's a piece of bone screeching under the scribing tool of the scrimshander.

4.

East of the Western Fence

And lo, the Rooster King, how he slums like the Lord!
And lo, the Rooster King, how he chases from these vacant lots the
    lesser, more domestic cocks!
And lo, the Rooster King, how he spreads, as gasoline,
His wings, O stained-glass butterfly!

             Even kicked to shit and broken
As the stars are bright, is he not the rocket and the rocket
Launcher? Does he not walk, as Caesar, robed
In lightning, his tail feathers,

Phosphorescent, flinging out
Like tracer fire? He is Fat Sam, the Feral Mariachi, the Ayatollah of
    Osceola,
The Phoenix of the Vinegar Works! He throbs
Like a cut throat and doesn't

             Bleed. And when he bleeds,
He bleeds whiskey—Fighting Cock: 103-Proof Kentucky Straight
Bourbon—O, world of light!
The light of the world:

Ruined. Magnificent; ferocious, florid—
So what. You think he's afraid of fire? He wasn't born, he was
    forged.
He's the napalm love letter, the sweetheart
Carpet bomb, the 1967 Pontiac

With a straight-6, single-barrel
Boot to the face. No ram unto
The shackle, this bantam assassin, his death-red hackles flaring
    like a funeral pyre.
He's the Sacred Heart of Jesus

Wound round with barbed wire, the crucifixion
Tattooed on the back of a contract killer.

Lo and
Behold—

5.

Cento

As when the cock crows on the left and all
His torn-out bloodied feathers drift down.

6.

Eye Against I

Low rock wall; a mocking-
Bird. A boy,

           Riding a bi-
Cycle. Sirens; some wind.

Rooster (crowing), banana
Tree, clothes-

           Line (clean
Sheets), chimney pipe, cat.

———————

Two chickens…, two *hens*
Scratching in

           The patchy
Grass of the lot across the

Street. A little bit of wind.
A little shaky

Sunlight in
The oleander; on the back

————

Deck, black pots of peach–
Petaled beach

Flower. A
Drunk lurches by, slurring

And kicking over garbage
Cans. Thunder.

The smell of
Cigar smoke—; star jasmine.

7.

Note to Self

A cool wet spring. Everything rotten.

8.

Dogs

Dogs pass no laws against you and knock not they your
    daughters up and do not to Manhattan go with your last two
    hundred dollars so, in general,
Dogs are A-OK with me. It's people should be neutered and
    kept off the grass. People
And cats. People—like cats—are mean and always breeding and
    make your teeth hurt.
Plus, they're sneaky. No dog caught dead would sneaking be and
    anyone says otherwise is a doggone,
Cat-loving liar. A dog can't
Tell a lie; a cat can't tell the truth; and people, at least the ones
    I've known, can't tell the difference. That's why I
Live alone. With my two dogs.
That—, and because everyone
Else is gone.

9.

Fat Sam Is Dead

Fat Sam is dead! King Cock is dead! O, fiery rooster!
Now who will, with hackled head, decide the skies? Who'll
    come a'crash like shrapnel, flapping, now?
O!—, Emperor of the Broken Neck! Strewn jewel!
It's not raining…, how is that possible? This slum
Groans like a calving glacier in your death's
Black wake.

                  Sir Bird—! Why did they murder you?
Why did you let them murder you? Now who will translate the
    wind into the language of the elderly
Women every time the sun strums his dumb
Harp?

10.

Today Is Sunday, the Emptiest of Days

Yesterday: manic. Today: subdued. To the west, thin wisps of cloud. Heidegger says, at the end of his "Letter on Humanism," that "language is the language of Being, as clouds are the clouds of the sky." I wonder what he meant by that. He also says "what is needed in the present world crisis is less philosophy, but more attentiveness in thinking." Sitting on my front porch, in my blue rocking chair, looking at the trash-strewn street, the ramshackled shotgun shacks collapsing in the shadow of the overpass, I do not wonder for an instant what he meant by that.

———

Last night: grumpy. This morning: cold and grumpy. The old woman who lives in the yellow house on the corner is gardening. Not much of a garden, really—just a bunch of empty flowerpots. Which is to say: the old woman who lives in the yellow house on the corner is rearranging a bunch of empty flowerpots. Her grandson is chasing some chickens up and down the street.

———

Dozing in my blue rocking chair on a porch lit by orchids, the sound of a cock crowing in the lot across the street—

———

Splitting headache (hung over), heavy overcast, a little cooler. Sat on my front porch and watched a house being built. Heard a rooster crowing and a bricklayer tapping his mason's trowel against a cinderblock. Günter Grass came to mind:

> Last week, the masons came
> Bringing with them what tools they needed.
> They walled him up, that cock
> We all wished would stop crowing—.
> So how is it we can still hear him?
> That voice—, it makes the soup grow cold.
> Shivering, we stand by and watch the hens
> As they peck apart the plaster.
> What do they need, the calcium?

———

Last week, when the mangled bodies of his brothers were dumped in the street, bloody, wrapped in newsprint, their horny feet protruding, he looked on as an emperor, hovering above the wings ripped from their sockets, the broken necks, the eyes strewn across the sidewalk—

———

"Don't outlive your usefulness," my father said, apropos of what I don't remember.

                                      A freight train whistles past

On its way to…where?

Father?

11.

Note to Self

                    On the red maple and the winged elm
The sun is setting, while on the spider flower and hollyhock,
The moon is just starting to throw its thin

Watery light. Two chickens, a threadbare cock and hen, have
      come to roost in the branches of a bottlebrush tree.
A squadron of dragonflies is darning the darkening

Yard. Correction: a squadron of dragonflies is darning the air
      above the darkening
Yard, closing up the holes the light is
Leaving—

12.

Note to Self

In the whisper-thin hiss of the wind
In the thickets, in the crow of the rooster and the trill of the
    crickets, a hint
Of all that's infinite is
Flitting, an indication, however small, of eternity—its dark
    heartbeat.

13.

So Many Birds to Kill and So Few Stones

How can a man who owns so little owe so much?

It rains for a while and then it doesn't. The phone rings. The pipes rattle. A breeze blows and the house settles. And when the cocks come, frugging and astrut, their gaudy plumage plashing brash against a backdrop of blocked-up cars and weedy lots and bank-owned cottages, their doors knocked heavy-off-the-hinge, one cannot help but flattened be by the persistence of the beautiful thing.

How a man who owns so little can owe so much—

It's cold. Overcast. Dreary. The day's weak light is trapped between the low clouds and the ground. It's falling from the bleak sky down, crashing into yellowed grass, broken glass, trash, the tin roofs of the shotgun shacks, then drifting, crippled, upward, stunned, to the low-slung dark eruptions of the clouds. Even in this underglow, how the roosters' feathers flare! Iridescent. Ember-flecked—. As if

By bloody starlight lit, or fire. Oily as joy.

Oily as joy? I don't see it, but say it so

and smiling up from every slick will be that face angelic that we'll find the day we quit this place and leave behind what seasick, heavy dread attends our waking. And our rest—.

If you can call it rest.

THE COAST ROAD

On nights like these, when the house is too quiet, I walk into
    the moonlit yard and listen.

The wind in the oak tree says: *nothing ever happens when you*
    want it to.
The crickets in the witchgrass say: *there will never be an end*
To this droning of the surf, no end to this drowning
Of the surfer.

The tired tread of traffic in the distance.

It's not what one listens to that matters,
But what one listens *for*—.

From the rafters of the back porch, the remnants of a vespiary
    are hanging,
Its gray walls stripped thin by poison
And last night's

Rain.

A bird takes flight. The moon ignites. The evening weeps
Its traffic lights—

Isn't there a bird, somewhere, whose call sounds like *i'msorry,*
    i'msorry?

What silence is there deep enough
To follow a cry like that?

NOTES

The epigraph is my translation of lines 49–55 of Rainer Maria Rilke's poem "Orpheus. Eurydike. Hermes."

"Not All Skeletons Are Museum Quality": the inspiration for the first section of this poem was a painting I saw in Galleria Nazionale d'Arte Antica in the Palazzo Corsini. The painting is an anonymous full-color reproduction of a black-and-white print by Jacques Callot. The original print is entitled "La Pendaison," and comes from the series *Les Grandes Misères de la guerre*. The reproduction is entitled "Malfattori Impiccati: da Jacques Callot."

"A Moral Victory Is Still a Defeat" is after Donald Justice.

"Excerpts from the Unabridged History of Rainfall": "laying heavy leather" is a fight term that means "to land hard punches." The sections entitled "After the German" (I, II, and III) are my translations of portions of "Vor dem Sommerregen," by Rainer Maria Rilke, "Camp 16," by Günter Eich, and "Der Gewitterabend," by Georg Trakl, respectively.

"The Ranges of Birds" is a found poem assembled from the descriptions of bird voices in *A Field Guide to the Birds East of the Rockies*, by Roger Tory Peterson.

"The Rooster King": the cento that is section 5 consists of a line from Wallace Stevens's poem "Notes Toward a Supreme Fiction" and a line from Elizabeth Bishop's poem "Roosters." Section 8 is after John Berryman's sixty-third "Dream Song." Section 9 is after the poem "Kaspar ist Tot," by Hans Arp. Section 10 is for Dana

Levin. The italicized lines in section 10 are my translation of the poem "Bauarbeiten," by Günter Grass.

"The Coast Road": "there will never be an end to this droning of the surf" comes from Wallace Stevens's poem "Fabliau of Florida."

ACKNOWLEDGMENTS

I am grateful to the editors of the following magazines and journals, in which some of the poems in this book first appeared: *American Poetry Review, Bayou, Colorado Review, Connotation Press: An Online Artifact, Faultline, The Hampton-Sydney Poetry Review, The Iowa Review, The Journal, The Kenyon Review, Kenyon Review Online, The Literary Review, The Mailer Review, The Morning News, The New Republic, Plume, Poetry Daily, Poetry International, POOL, Puerto del Sol, The Seattle Review, Slate, Smartish Pace, Subtropics, Sugar House Review, The Wallace Stevens Journal,* and *Whiskey Island Magazine.*

Part 2 of "Umbrian Anecdotes" and "Alarums. Flourishes. Exeunt." were reprinted in *The World Is Charged: Poetic Engagements with Gerard Manley Hopkins,* edited by Daniel Westover and William Wright.

Thank you: T. Corey Brennan, Casey Lance Brown, Christopher Celenza, Katie Ford, Louise Glück, Stephanie Malia Hom, Kimberly Johnson, Aparna Keshaviah, Karl Kirchwey, Dominic Luxford, Jesse Nathan, Pina Pasquantonio, Cristina Puglisi, Paul Rudy, Adele Chatfield-Taylor, and Tyler Travillian.

I am indebted to the American Academy of Arts and Letters, the American Academy in Rome, the Lannan Foundation, and the Mrs. Giles Whiting Foundation, without whose generous support this book could not have been written.

ABOUT THE AUTHOR

Jay Hopler is the author of *Green Squall* and the editor (with Kimberly Johnson) of *Before the Door of God: An Anthology of Devotional Poetry*. The recipient of, among others, the Yale Series of Younger Poets Award, the Great Lakes Colleges Association New Writers Award, a fellowship from the Lannan Foundation, the Whiting Writers' Award, and the Rome Prize in Literature, he teaches in the writing program at the University of South Florida.

THE McSWEENEY'S POETRY SERIES

1. *Love, an Index* by Rebecca Lindenberg (2012).

2. *Fragile Acts* by Allan Peterson (2012).

3. *City of Rivers* by Zubair Ahmed (2012).

4. *x* by Dan Chelotti (2013).

5. *The Boss* by Victoria Chang (2013).

6. *TOMBO* by W. S. Di Piero (2014).

7. *Morning in Serra Mattu: A Nubian Ode* by Arif Gamal (2014).

8. *Saint Friend* by Carl Adamshick (2014).

9. *Tradition* by Daniel Khalastchi (2015).

10. *Remains* by Jesús Castillo (2016).

11. *Whosoever Has Let a Minotaur Enter Them, or a Sonnet—* by Emily Carr (2016).

12. *The Abridged History of Rainfall* by Jay Hopler (2016).